JAZZ PLAY ALONG®

Book and CD for B♭, E♭, C and Bass Clef Instruments

volume 75

Arranged and Produced by Mark Taylor and Jim Roberts

Paul DESMOND

10 JAZZ FAVORITES

BOOK

TITLE	PAGE NUMBERS C Treble Instruments	B♭ Instruments	E♭ Instruments	C Bass Instruments
All the Things You Are	4	21	38	55
Easy Living	6	22	40	56
Jeruvian	8	24	42	58
Rude Old Man	5	26	39	60
Samba Cantina	10	28	44	62
Samba De Orfeu	12	30	46	64
Suicide Is Painless (Song from M*A*S*H)	20	27	54	61
Take Five	14	32	48	66
Take Ten	16	34	50	68
When Joanna Loved Me	18	36	52	70

T0071406

CD

TITLE	CD Track Number Split Track / Melody	CD Track Number Full Stereo Track
All the Things You Are	1	2
Easy Living	3	4
Jeruvian	5	6
Rude Old Man	7	8
Samba Cantina	9	10
Samba De Orfeu	11	12
Suicide Is Painless (Song from M*A*S*H)	13	14
Take Five	15	16
Take Ten	17	18
When Joanna Loved Me	19	20
B♭ Tuning Notes		21

Cover photo © Gai Terrell / Redferns / Retna Ltd.

ISBN 13: 978-1-4234-2628-8
ISBN 10: 1-4234-2628-2

HAL•LEONARD® CORPORATION
7777 W. BLUEMOUND RD. P.O. BOX 13819 MILWAUKEE, WI 53213

Visit Hal Leonard Online at
www.halleonard.com

Paul Desmond

Volume 75

Arranged and Produced by
Mark Taylor and Jim Roberts

Featured Players:

John Desalme–Saxophones
Tony Nalker–Piano
Jim Roberts–Bass
Dave McDonald–Drums

Recorded at Bias Studios, Springfield, Virginia
Bob Dawson, Engineer

HOW TO USE THE CD:

Each song has two tracks:

1) Split Track/Melody

Woodwind, Brass, Keyboard, and **Mallet Players** can use this track as a learning tool for melody style and inflection.

Bass Players can learn and perform with this track – remove the recorded bass track by turning down the volume on the LEFT channel.

Keyboard and **Guitar Players** can learn and perform with this track – remove the recorded piano part by turning down the volume on the RIGHT channel.

2) Full Stereo Track

Soloists or **Groups** can learn and perform with this accompaniment track with the RHYTHM SECTION only.

CD
1 : SPLIT TRACK/MELODY
2 : FULL STEREO TRACK

ALL THE THINGS YOU ARE

FROM VERY WARM FOR MAY

LYRICS BY OSCAR HAMMERSTEIN II
MUSIC BY JEROME KERN

CD

7 : SPLIT TRACK/MELODY
8 : FULL STEREO TRACK

C VERSION

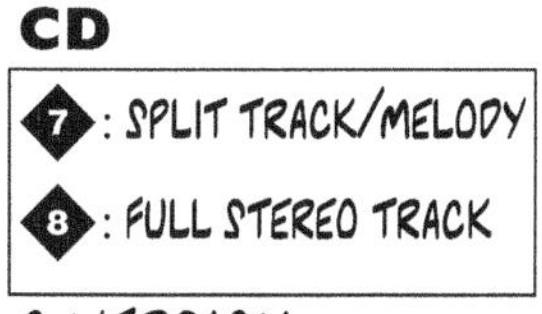

RUDE OLD MAN

BY EUGENE WRIGHT

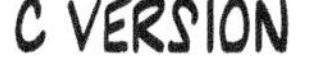

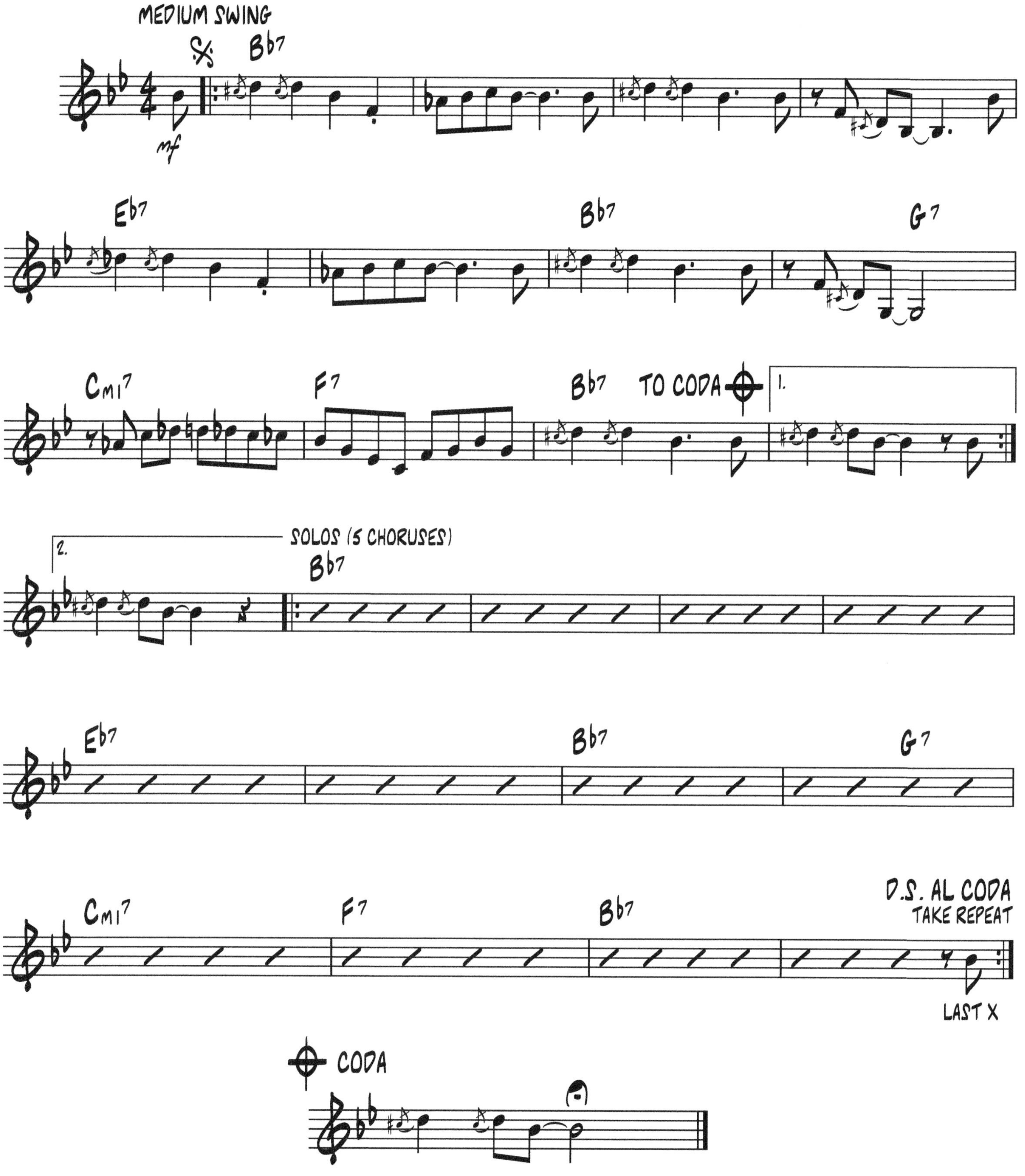
MEDIUM SWING
Bb7
mf
Eb7
Bb7
G7
Cmi7
F7
Bb7
TO CODA
1.
2.
SOLOS (5 CHORUSES)
Bb7
Eb7
Bb7
G7
Cmi7
F7
Bb7
D.S. AL CODA
TAKE REPEAT
LAST X
CODA

EASY LIVING

THEME FROM THE PARAMOUNT PICTURE EASY LIVING

WORDS AND MUSIC BY LEO ROBIN
AND RALPH RAINGER

CD
3 : SPLIT TRACK/MELODY
4 : FULL STEREO TRACK

C VERSION

FMI7 Bb7 FMI7 BMI7 E7(b9)
EbMA7 GMI7(b5) C7(b9) FMI7 AMI7(b5) D7(b9)
GMI7 BbMI7 A7(b5) AbMA7 AbMI7 Db7
GMI7 C7 FMI7 Bb7 TO CODA
Eb6 C7(b9) FMI7 Bb7 SOLO EbMA7 GMI7(b5) C7(b9) FMI7 AMI7(b5) D7(b9)
GMI7 BbMI7 A7(b5) AbMA7 AbMI7 Db7 GMI7 C7 FMI7 Bb7
GMI7 C7(b9) FMI7 Bb7 EbMA7 GMI7(b5) C7(b9) FMI7 AMI7(b5) D7(b9)
GMI7 BbMI7 A7(b5) AbMA7 AbMI7 Db7 GMI7 C7 FMI7 Bb7
D.S. AL CODA
Eb6 DbMI7 Gb7
CODA
EbMA7 Db7
Cb7 Bb7 Cb7 Bb7 EbMA7

CD

5 : SPLIT TRACK/MELODY

6 : FULL STEREO TRACK

JERUVIAN

BY DAVE VAN KRIEDT

C VERSION

SOLOS (2 CHORUSES)
AbMA7 Bb7 BbMI7 Eb7 AbMA7
1ST X ONLY
EbMI7 Ab7 DbMA7 Gb7 C7 F+7 BbMI7 Eb7
AbMA7 Bb7 BbMI7 Eb7 AbMA7
EbMI7 Ab7 DbMA7 Gb7 C7 F+7 Bb7 Eb7
GMA7 BMI7 E7 AMA7 C#MI7 F#7
BMA7 BbMI7 Eb7 CMI7 F7(b9) BbMI7 Eb7(b9)
AbMA7 Bb7 BbMI7 Eb7 AbMA7
D.C. AL CODA
EbMI7 Ab7 DbMA7 Gb7 C7 F+7 BbMI7 Eb7
CODA BbMI7 AMA7 AbMA7
3

CD

9: SPLIT TRACK/MELODY
10: FULL STEREO TRACK

C VERSION

SAMBA CANTINA

BY PAUL DESMOND

TO CODA
Bbmi7 /Ab Gmi7(b5) C7 Fmi7 /Eb Bb7/D Bbmi6/Db
C7sus Fmi7 Ab7
SOLO
Gmi7(b5) C7 Fmi7 Bbmi7 Eb7
Abma7 Gmi7(b5) C7 Fmi7
Dmi7(b5) G7 C7 Ab7 Gmi7(b5) C7
Fmi7 Bbmi7 Eb7 Cmi7 F7
Bbmi7 /Ab Gmi7(b5) C7 Fmi7 /Eb Bb7/D Bbmi6/Db
C7sus C7(b9) Fmi7
D.S. AL CODA
3
CODA
C7sus C7(b9) Fmi7 Fmi6 Fmi7
Fmi6 Fmi7 Fmi6 Fmi7 Fmi6/9

CD

11 : SPLIT TRACK/MELODY
12 : FULL STEREO TRACK

C VERSION

SAMBA DE ORFEU

WORDS BY ANTONIO MARIA
MUSIC BY LUIZ BONFA

FMI7
Bb7
3
EbMI7
Ab7
EbMI7
Ab7SUS
Ab7
TO CODA
EbMI7
Ab7
DbMA7
SOLO
DbMA7
FMI7
Bb7
EbMI7
Ab7
EbMI7
Ab7SUS
Ab7
EbMI7
Ab7
1.
DbMA7
Ab7SUS
2.
DbMA7
AbMI7
Db7
GbMA7
F#MI7
B7
FMI7
Bb7
EbMI7
Ab7SUS
DbMA7
FMI7
Bb7
EbMI7
Ab7
EbMI7
Ab7SUS
Ab7
EbMI7
Ab7
DbMA7
D.S. AL CODA
CODA
EbMI7
Ab7
Db6/9
Ab7SUS
Db6/9
Ab7SUS
Db6/9
Ab7SUS
DbMA7

C VERSION

TAKE FIVE

BY PAUL DESMOND

MEDIUM SWING

Ebmi Bbmi7 Ebmi Bbmi7 Ebmi Bbmi7 Ebmi Bbmi7

RHYTHM

mf

Ebmi Bbmi7 Ebmi Bbmi7 Ebmi Bbmi7 Ebmi Bbmi7

Ebmi Bbmi7 Ebmi Bbmi7 Ebmi Bbmi7 Cbma7

Bbmi7 Abmi7 Gbma7

Cbma7 Bbmi7 Abmi7 Fmi7(b5) Bb7(b9)

Ebmi Bbmi7 Ebmi Bbmi7 Ebmi Bbmi7 Ebmi Bbmi7

TO CODA

Ebmi Bbmi7 Ebmi Bbmi7 Ebmi Bbmi7 Ebmi Bbmi7

SOLO
D.S. AL CODA
CODA

CD

17: SPLIT TRACK/MELODY

18: FULL STEREO TRACK

TAKE TEN

BY PAUL DESMOND

C VERSION

DMI7 G7 | DMI7 G7 | DMI7 G7

DMI7 G7 | DMI7 G7 | DMI7 G7 | DMI7 G7

TO CODA

SOLO

DMI7 G7 | DMI7 G7 | DMI7 G7 | DMI7 G7

DMI7 G7 | DMI7 G7 | DMI7 G7 | DMI7 G7

Bb MI7 Eb7 | Ab MA7 F7 | Bb MI7 Eb7 | Ab MA7

GMI7 C7 | FMA7 D7 | GMI7 C7 | EMI7 A7

DMI7 G7 | DMI7 G7 | DMI7 G7 | DMI7 G7

D.S. AL CODA

DMI7 G7 | DMI7 G7 | DMI7 G7 | DMI7 G7

CODA

DMI7 G7 | DMI7 G7 | DMI7 G7 | DMI7 G7

DMI7 G7 | DMI7 G7 | DMI7 G7 | DMI7

CD

19 : SPLIT TRACK/MELODY

20 : FULL STEREO TRACK

WHEN JOANNA LOVED ME

WORDS AND MUSIC BY ROBERT WELLS
AND JACK SEGAL

C VERSION

Eb MA7
Gm17
C7(b9)
SOLO
Fm17
Bb7
Fm17(b5)/Cb
Bbm17
Eb7
Ab MA7
Abm17
A7
D7
C7
Bb7(b9)
E7
RIT.

CD

13 : SPLIT TRACK/MELODY
14 : FULL STEREO TRACK

SUICIDE IS PAINLESS

(SONG FROM M*A*S*H)

WORDS AND MUSIC BY MIKE ALTMAN
AND JOHNNY MANDEL

C VERSION

MEDIUM ROCK BALLAD

CD

1 : SPLIT TRACK/MELODY

2 : FULL STEREO TRACK

ALL THE THINGS YOU ARE

FROM VERY WARM FOR MAY

LYRICS BY OSCAR HAMMERSTEIN II
MUSIC BY JEROME KERN

B♭ VERSION

CD

3: SPLIT TRACK/MELODY

4: FULL STEREO TRACK

EASY LIVING

THEME FROM THE PARAMOUNT PICTURE EASY LIVING

WORDS AND MUSIC BY LEO ROBIN
AND RALPH RAINGER

B♭ VERSION

GMI7 C7 GMI7 C#MI7 F#7(b9)
FMA7 AMI7(b5) D7(b9) GMI7 BMI7(b5) E7(b9)
AMI7 CMI7 B7(b5) BbMA7 BbMI7 Eb7
AMI7 D7 GMI7 C7
TO CODA
F6 D7(b9) GMI7 C7
SOLO
FMA7 AMI7(b5) D7(b9) GMI7 BMI7(b5) E7(b9)
AMI7 CMI7 B7(b5) BbMA7 BbMI7 Eb7 AMI7 D7 GMI7 C7
AMI7 D7(b9) GMI7 C7 FMA7 AMI7(b5) D7(b9) GMI7 BMI7(b5) E7(b9)
AMI7 CMI7 B7(b5) BbMA7 BbMI7 Eb7 AMI7 D7 GMI7 C7
D.S. AL CODA
F6 EbMI7 Ab7
CODA
FMA7 Eb7
Db7 C7 Db7 C7 FMA7

CD

5: SPLIT TRACK/MELODY
6: FULL STEREO TRACK

JERUVIAN

BY DAVE VAN KRIEDT

B♭ VERSION

SOLOS (2 CHORUSES)
1ST X ONLY
D.C. AL CODA
CODA

CD

7: SPLIT TRACK/MELODY
8: FULL STEREO TRACK

RUDE OLD MAN

BY EUGENE WRIGHT

B♭ VERSION

CD
13 : SPLIT TRACK/MELODY
14 : FULL STEREO TRACK
SUICIDE IS PAINLESS
(SONG FROM M*A*S*H)
WORDS AND MUSIC BY MIKE ALTMAN
AND JOHNNY MANDEL
B♭ VERSION
MEDIUM ROCK BALLAD
EMI7
PLAY
PIANO
mf
AMI7 D7 BMI7 EMI7 AMI7
D7 GMA7 EMI7 E7 AMI7
D7SUS BMI7 EMI7 CMA7 BMI7 AMI7 D7SUS
EMI7
TO CODA
SOLOS (2 CHORUSES)
AMI7 D7 BMI7 EMI7 AMI7
D7 EMI7 E7 AMI7 D7SUS BMI7 EMI7
CMA7 BMI7 AMI7 D7SUS EMI7 EMI7
D.S. AL CODA
LAST X
CODA
PIANO

CD

9 : SPLIT TRACK/MELODY
10 : FULL STEREO TRACK

SAMBA CANTINA

BY PAUL DESMOND

B♭ VERSION

TO CODA
Cmi7 /Bb Ami7(b5) D7 Gmi7 /F C7/E Cmi6/Eb
D7SUS Gmi7 Bb7
SOLO
Ami7(b5) D7 Gmi7 Cmi7 F7
Bbma7 Ami7(b5) D7 Gmi7
Emi7(b5) A7 D7 Bb7 Ami7(b5) D7
Gmi7 Cmi7 F7 Dmi7 G7
Cmi7 /Bb Ami7(b5) D7 Gmi7 /F C7/E Cmi6/Eb
D7SUS D7(b9) Gmi7
D.S. AL CODA
3
CODA
D7SUS D7(b9) Gmi7 Gmi6 Gmi7
Gmi6 Gmi7 Gmi6 Gmi7 Gmi6/9

CD

11 : SPLIT TRACK/MELODY
12 : FULL STEREO TRACK

SAMBA DE ORFEU

WORDS BY ANTONIO MARIA
MUSIC BY LUIZ BONFA

B♭ VERSION

GMI7 C7 FMI7
Bb7 FMI7 Bb7SUS Bb7 TO CODA
FMI7 Bb7 EbMA7
SOLO
EbMA7 GMI7 C7 FMI7
Bb7 FMI7 Bb7SUS Bb7 FMI7
Bb7 1. EbMA7 Bb7SUS 2. EbMA7 BbMI7 Eb7
AbMA7 G#MI7 C#7 GMI7 C7 FMI7 Bb7SUS EbMA7
GMI7 C7 FMI7 Bb7 FMI7
Bb7SUS Bb7 FMI7 Bb7 EbMA7 D.S. AL CODA
CODA
FMI7 Bb7 Eb6/9 Bb7SUS
Eb6/9 Bb7SUS Eb6/9 Bb7SUS EbMA7

CD

15: SPLIT TRACK/MELODY
16: FULL STEREO TRACK

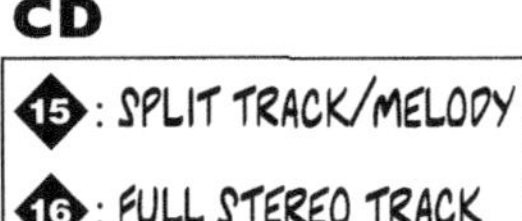

TAKE FIVE

BY PAUL DESMOND

B♭ VERSION

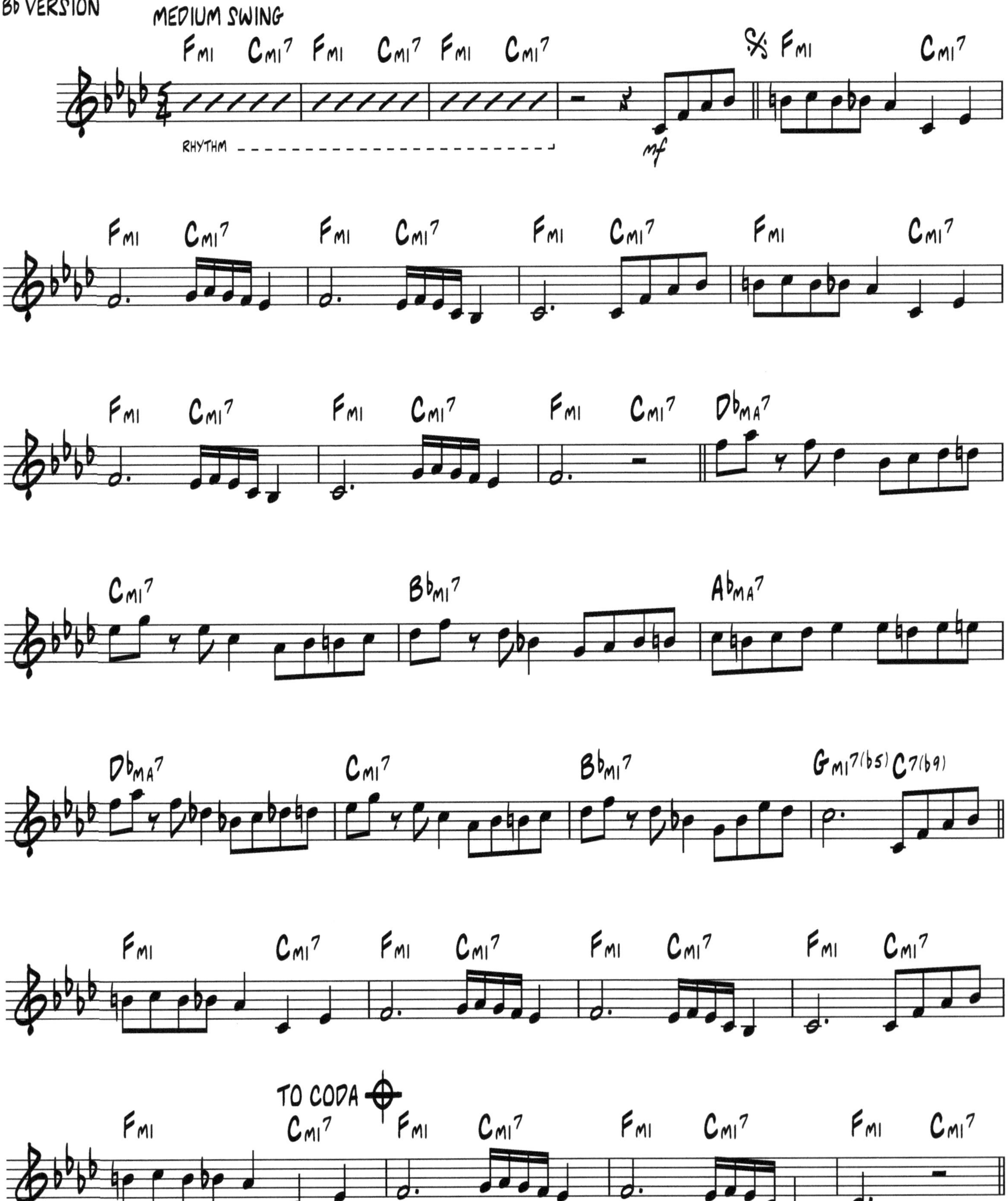
MEDIUM SWING
FMI CMI7 FMI CMI7 FMI CMI7
RHYTHM
mf
FMI CMI7
FMI CMI7 FMI CMI7 FMI CMI7 FMI CMI7
FMI CMI7 FMI CMI7 FMI CMI7 D♭MA7
CMI7 B♭MI7 A♭MA7
D♭MA7 CMI7 B♭MI7 GMI7(♭5) C7(♭9)
FMI CMI7 FMI CMI7 FMI CMI7 FMI CMI7
TO CODA
FMI CMI7 FMI CMI7 FMI CMI7 FMI CMI7

SOLO
FMI CMI7 FMI CMI7 FMI CMI7 FMI CMI7
FMI CMI7 FMI CMI7 FMI CMI7 FMI CMI7
D♭MA7 CMI7 B♭MI7 A♭MA7 D♭MA7
CMI7 B♭MI7 GMI7(♭5) FMI CMI7
FMI CMI7 FMI CMI7 FMI CMI7 FMI CMI7 FMI CMI7
D.S. AL CODA
FMI CMI7 FMI CMI7
CODA
FMI CMI7 FMI CMI7
FMI CMI7 FMI CMI7 FMI CMI7 FMI CMI7 FMI CMI7
FMI CMI7 FMI CMI7 FMI CMI7 FMI CMI7 FMI

CD

17: SPLIT TRACK/MELODY
18: FULL STEREO TRACK

TAKE TEN

BY PAUL DESMOND

B♭ VERSION

EMI7 A7 EMI7 A7 EMI7 A7
TO CODA
EMI7 A7 EMI7 A7 EMI7 A7 EMI7 A7
SOLO
EMI7 A7 EMI7 A7 EMI7 A7 EMI7 A7
EMI7 A7 EMI7 A7 EMI7 A7 EMI7 A7
CMI7 F7 Bb MA7 G7 CMI7 F7 Bb MA7
AMI7 D7 GMA7 E7 AMI7 D7 F#MI7 B7
EMI7 A7 EMI7 A7 EMI7 A7 EMI7 A7
D.S. AL CODA
EMI7 A7 EMI7 A7 EMI7 A7 EMI7 A7
CODA
EMI7 A7 EMI7 A7 EMI7 A7 EMI7 A7
EMI7 A7 EMI7 A7 EMI7 A7 EMI7

CD

19: SPLIT TRACK/MELODY
20: FULL STEREO TRACK

WHEN JOANNA LOVED ME

WORDS AND MUSIC BY ROBERT WELLS
AND JACK SEGAL

B♭ VERSION MEDIUM SWING

FMA7
AMI7
D7(b9)
SOLO
GMI7
C7
GMI7(b5)/Db
CMI7
F7
BbMA7
BbMI7
B7
E7
D7
C7(b9)
F#7
RIT.

CD

ALL THE THINGS YOU ARE

FROM VERY WARM FOR MAY

LYRICS BY OSCAR HAMMERSTEIN II
MUSIC BY JEROME KERN

CD

7 : SPLIT TRACK/MELODY
8 : FULL STEREO TRACK

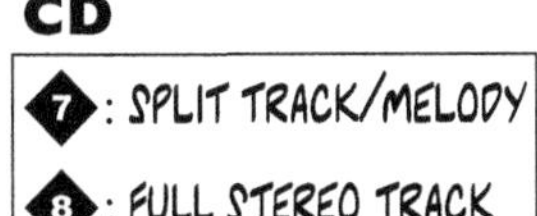

RUDE OLD MAN

BY EUGENE WRIGHT

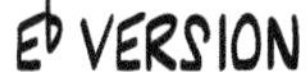

E♭ VERSION

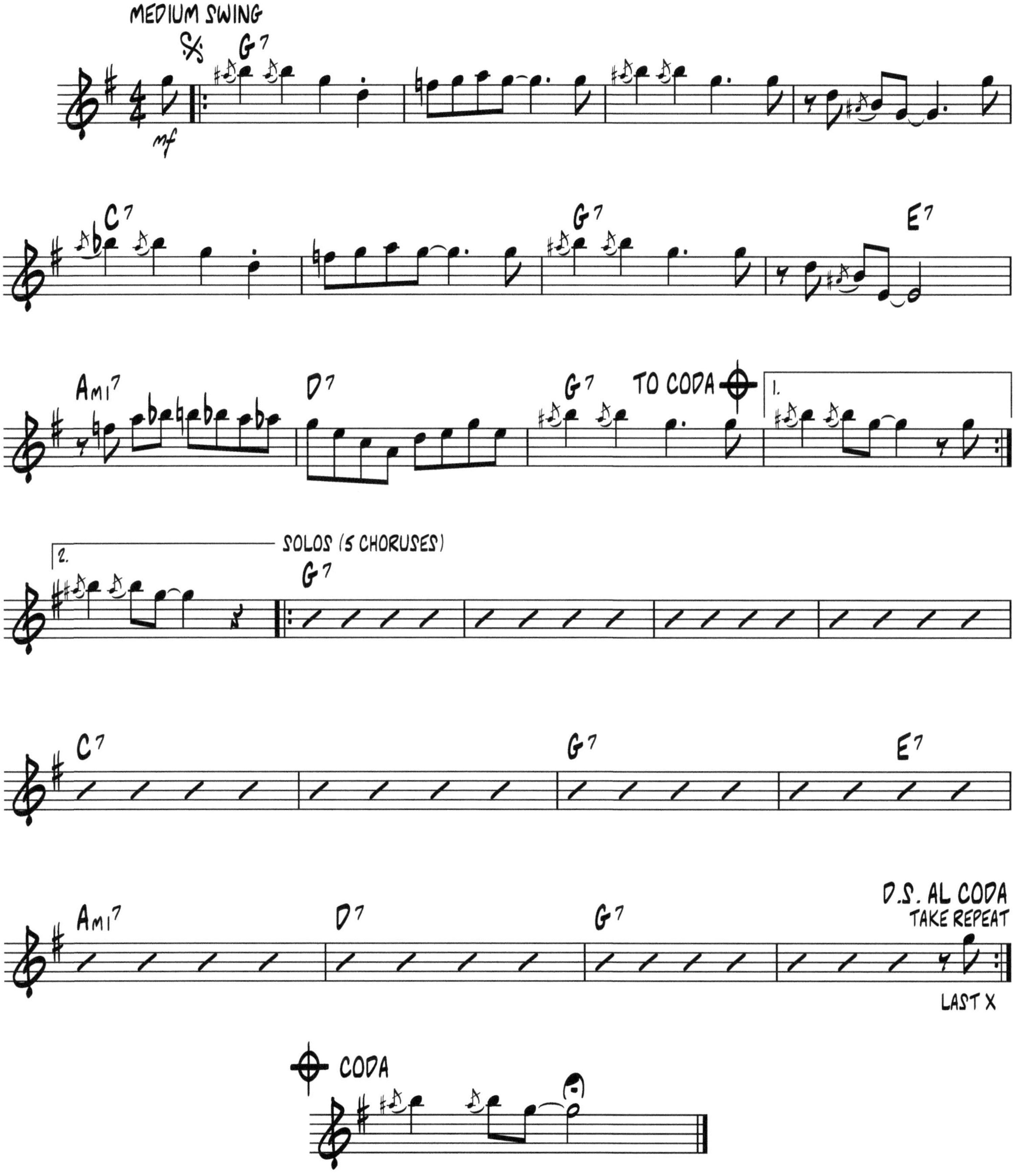

MEDIUM SWING
G7
mf
C7
G7
E7
Ami7
D7
G7
TO CODA
1.
2.
SOLOS (5 CHORUSES)
G7
C7
G7
E7
Ami7
D7
G7
D.S. AL CODA
TAKE REPEAT
LAST X
CODA

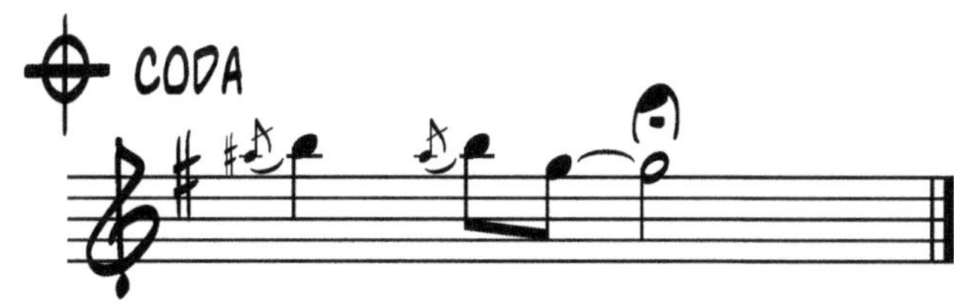

EASY LIVING

THEME FROM THE PARAMOUNT PICTURE EASY LIVING

WORDS AND MUSIC BY LEO ROBIN
AND RALPH RAINGER

DMI7 G7 DMI7 G#MI7 C#7(b9)
CMA7 EMI7(b5) A7(b9) DMI7 F#MI7(b5) B7(b9)
EMI7 GMI7 F#7(b5) FMA7 FMI7 Bb7
EMI7 A7 DMI7 G7
TO CODA
SOLO
C6 A7(b9) DMI7 G7 CMA7 EMI7(b5) A7(b9) DMI7 F#MI7(b5) B7(b9)
EMI7 GMI7 F#7(b5) FMA7 FMI7 Bb7 EMI7 A7 DMI7 G7
EMI7 A7(b9) DMI7 G7 CMA7 EMI7(b5) A7(b9) DMI7 F#MI7(b5) B7(b9)
EMI7 GMI7 F#7(b5) FMA7 FMI7 Bb7 EMI7 A7 DMI7 G7
D.S. AL CODA
C6 BbMI7 Eb7
CODA
CMA7 Bb7
Ab7 G7 Ab7 G7 CMA7

CD

5 : SPLIT TRACK/MELODY
6 : FULL STEREO TRACK

JERUVIAN

BY DAVE VAN KRIEDT

SOLOS (2 CHORUSES)
FMA7
G7
GMI7
C7
FMA7
1ST X ONLY
CMI7
F7
Bbma7
Eb7
A7
D+7
GMI7
C7
EMA7
G#MI7
C#7
F#MA7
A#MI7
D#7
G#MA7
AMI7
D7(b9)
C7(b9)
D.C. AL CODA
CODA
F#MA7

CD

- 9 : SPLIT TRACK/MELODY
- 10 : FULL STEREO TRACK

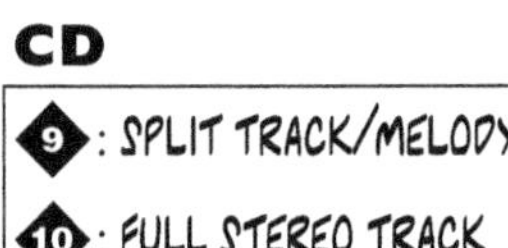

SAMBA CANTINA

BY PAUL DESMOND

E♭ VERSION

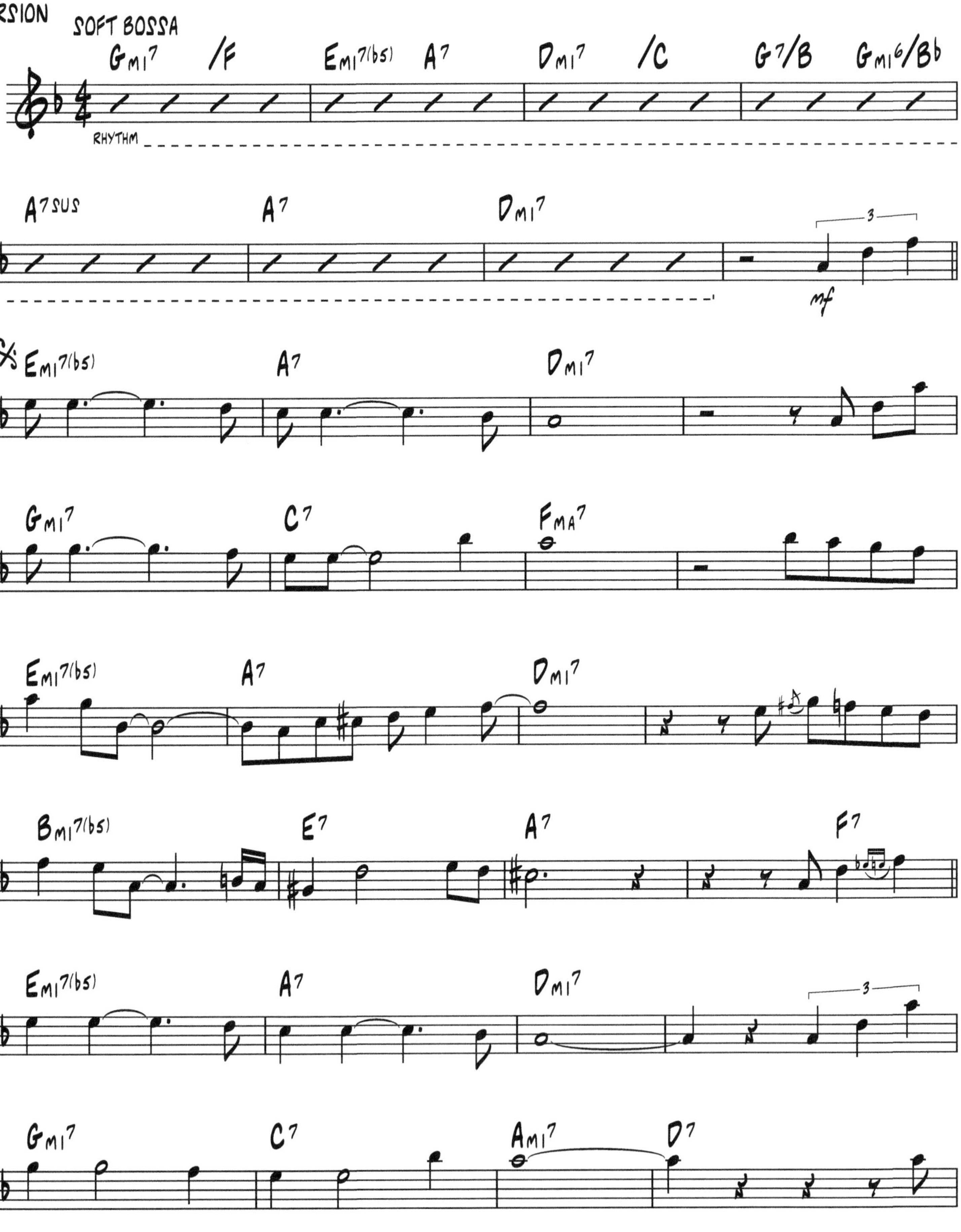
SOFT BOSSA
GMI7 /F EMI7(♭5) A7 DMI7 /C G7/B GMI6/B♭
RHYTHM
A7SUS A7 DMI7
3
mf
EMI7(♭5) A7 DMI7
GMI7 C7 FMA7
EMI7(♭5) A7 DMI7
BMI7(♭5) E7 A7 F7
EMI7(♭5) A7 DMI7
3
GMI7 C7 AMI7 D7

TO CODA
Gmi7 /F Emi7(b5) A7 Dmi7 /C G7/B Gmi6/Bb
A7sus
Dmi7
F7
SOLO
Emi7(b5) A7 Dmi7 Gmi7 C7
Fma7 Emi7(b5) A7 Dmi7
Bmi7(b5) E7 A7 F7 Emi7(b5) A7
Dmi7 Gmi7 C7 Ami7 D7
Gmi7 /F Emi7(b5) A7 Dmi7 /C G7/B Gmi6/Bb
A7sus A7(b9) Dmi7
D.S. AL CODA
3
CODA
A7sus A7(b9) Dmi7 Dmi6 Dmi7
Dmi6 Dmi7 Dmi6 Dmi7 Dmi6/9

CD

11 : SPLIT TRACK/MELODY
12 : FULL STEREO TRACK

SAMBA DE ORFEU

WORDS BY ANTONIO MARIA
MUSIC BY LUIZ BONFA

E♭ VERSION

DMI7
G7
CMI7
F7
CMI7
F7SUS
F7
TO CODA
CMI7
F7
B♭MA7
SOLO
B♭MA7
DMI7
G7
CMI7
F7
CMI7
F7SUS
F7
CMI7
F7
B♭MA7
F7SUS
B♭MA7
FMI7
B♭7
E♭MA7
D♯MI7
G♯7
DMI7 G7
CMI7 F7SUS
B♭MA7
DMI7
G7
CMI7
F7
CMI7
F7SUS
F7
CMI7
F7
B♭MA7
D.S. AL CODA
CODA
CMI7
F7
B♭6/9
F7SUS
B♭6/9
F7SUS
B♭6/9
F7SUS
B♭MA7

CD

15: SPLIT TRACK/MELODY
16: FULL STEREO TRACK

TAKE FIVE

BY PAUL DESMOND

E♭ VERSION

SOLO
CMI GMI7 CMI GMI7 CMI GMI7 CMI GMI7
CMI GMI7 CMI GMI7 CMI GMI7 CMI GMI7
AbMA7 GMI7 FMI7 EbMA7 AbMA7
GMI7 FMI7 DMI7(b5) CMI GMI7
CMI GMI7 CMI GMI7 CMI GMI7 CMI GMI7 CMI GMI7
D.S. AL CODA
CMI GMI7 CMI GMI7
CODA
CMI GMI7 CMI GMI7
CMI GMI7 CMI GMI7 CMI GMI7 CMI GMI7 CMI GMI7
CMI GMI7 CMI GMI7 CMI GMI7 CMI GMI7 CMI

CD

17 : SPLIT TRACK/MELODY

18 : FULL STEREO TRACK

TAKE TEN

BY PAUL DESMOND

E♭ VERSION

BMI7 E7 BMI7 E7 BMI7 E7

BMI7 E7 BMI7 E7 BMI7 E7 TO CODA BMI7 E7

SOLO

BMI7 E7 BMI7 E7 BMI7 E7 BMI7 E7

BMI7 E7 BMI7 E7 BMI7 E7 BMI7 E7

GMI7 C7 FMA7 D7 GMI7 C7 FMA7

EMI7 A7 DMA7 B7 EMI7 A7 C#MI7 F#7

BMI7 E7 BMI7 E7 BMI7 E7 BMI7 E7

D.S. AL CODA

BMI7 E7 BMI7 E7 BMI7 E7 BMI7 E7

CODA

BMI7 E7 BMI7 E7 BMI7 E7 BMI7 E7

BMI7 E7 BMI7 E7 BMI7 E7 BMI7

CD

19 : SPLIT TRACK/MELODY
20 : FULL STEREO TRACK

WHEN JOANNA LOVED ME

WORDS AND MUSIC BY ROBERT WELLS
AND JACK SEGAL

E♭ VERSION

CMA7
EMI7
A7(b9)
SOLO
DMI7
G7
CMA7
EMI7
A7(b9)
DMI7
G7
CMA7
EMI7
A7(b9)
DMI7
G7
CMA7
EMI7
A7(b9)
DMI7
DMI7(b5)/Ab
GMI7
C7
FMA7
FMI7
CMA7
F#7
B7
EMI7
A7
DMI7
G7
DMI7
G7
CMA7
EMI7
A7(b9)
DMI7
G7(b9)
CMA7
C#7
CMA7
RIT.

CD

13: SPLIT TRACK/MELODY

14: FULL STEREO TRACK

SUICIDE IS PAINLESS

(SONG FROM M*A*S*H)

WORDS AND MUSIC BY MIKE ALTMAN
AND JOHNNY MANDEL

E♭ VERSION

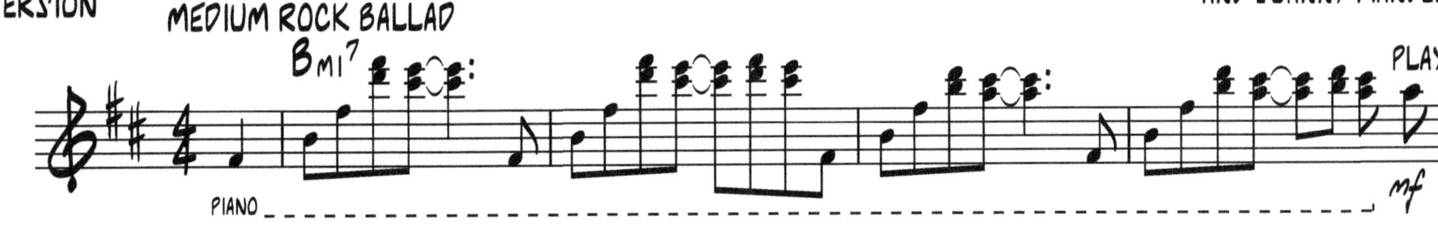

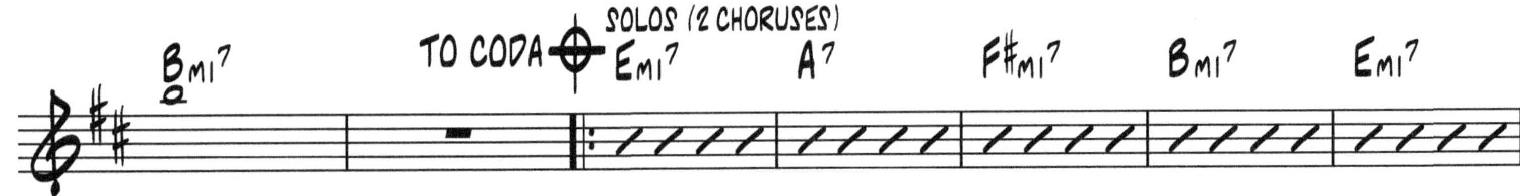

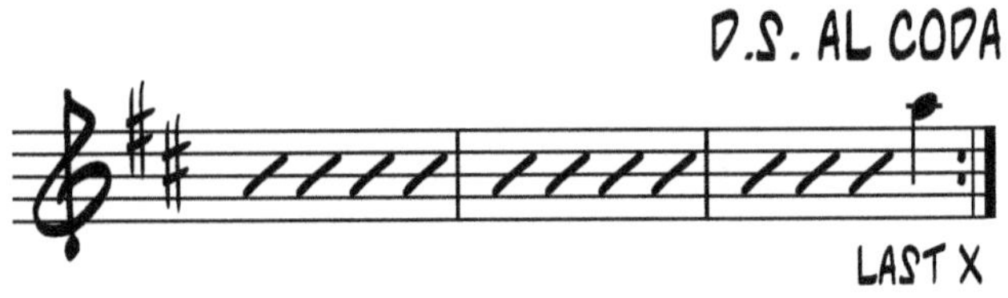

ALL THE THINGS YOU ARE

FROM VERY WARM FOR MAY

LYRICS BY OSCAR HAMMERSTEIN II
MUSIC BY JEROME KERN

CD
3 : SPLIT TRACK/MELODY
4 : FULL STEREO TRACK
EASY LIVING
THEME FROM THE PARAMOUNT PICTURE EASY LIVING
WORDS AND MUSIC BY LEO ROBIN
AND RALPH RAINGER
C VERSION
SLOW SWING
mf

FMI7 Bb7 FMI7 BMI7 E7(b9)
EbMA7 GMI7(b5) C7(b9) FMI7 AMI7(b5) D7(b9)
GMI7 BbMI7 A7(b5) AbMA7 AbMI7 Db7
GMI7 C7 FMI7 Bb7
TO CODA
SOLO
Eb6 C7(b9) FMI7 Bb7 EbMA7 GMI7(b5) C7(b9) FMI7 AMI7(b5) D7(b9)
GMI7 BbMI7 A7(b5) AbMA7 AbMI7 Db7 GMI7 C7 FMI7 Bb7
GMI7 C7(b9) FMI7 Bb7 EbMA7 GMI7(b5) C7(b9) FMI7 AMI7(b5) D7(b9)
GMI7 BbMI7 A7(b5) AbMA7 AbMI7 Db7 GMI7 C7 FMI7 Bb7
D.S. AL CODA
Eb6 DbMI7 Gb7
CODA
EbMA7 Db7
Cb7 Bb7 Cb7 Bb7 EbMA7

CD

5: SPLIT TRACK/MELODY
6: FULL STEREO TRACK

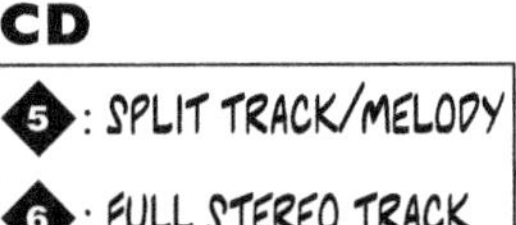

JERUVIAN

BY DAVE VAN KRIEDT

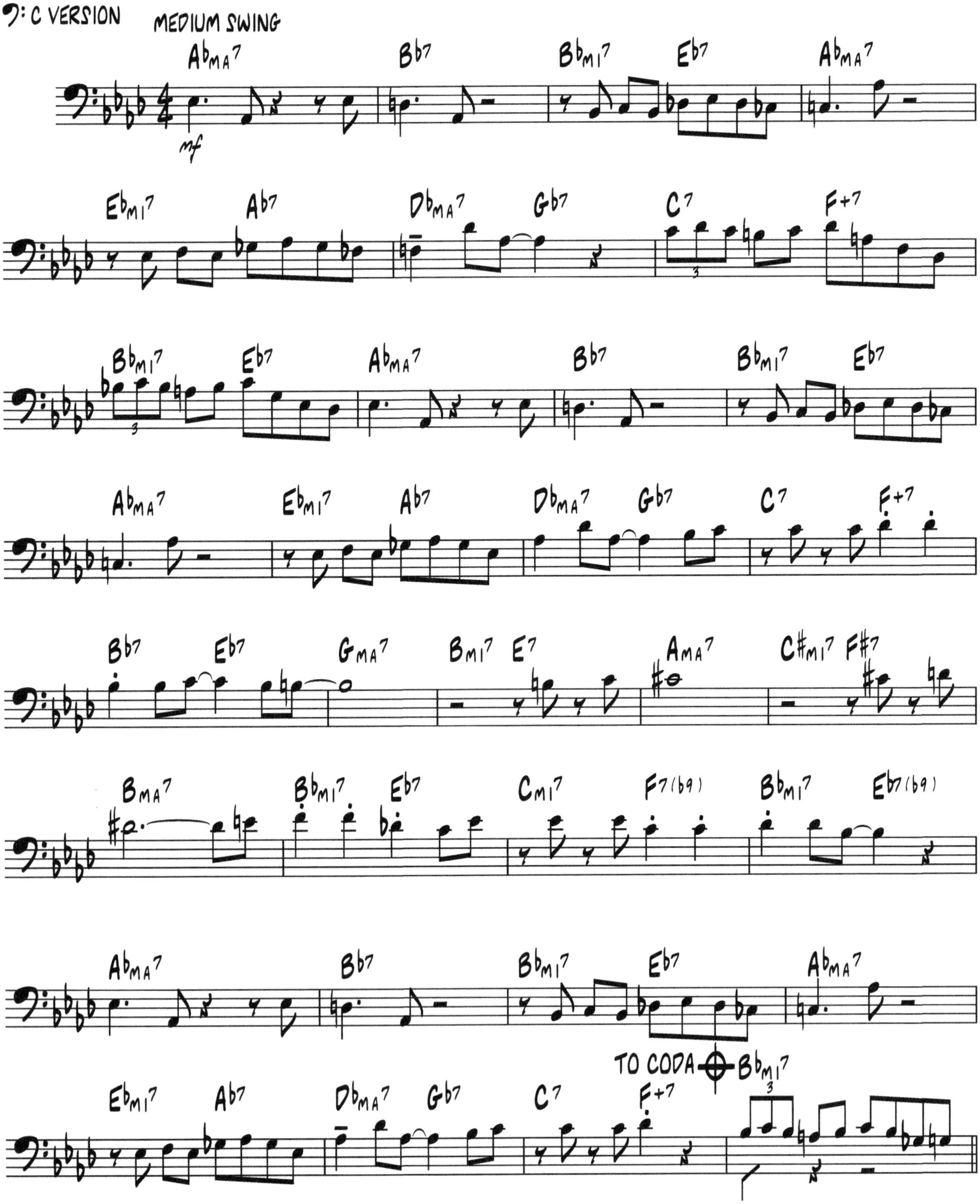
C VERSION
MEDIUM SWING
AbMA7 Bb7 BbMI7 Eb7 AbMA7
mf
EbMI7 Ab7 DbMA7 Gb7 C7 F+7
BbMI7 Eb7 AbMA7 Bb7 BbMI7 Eb7
AbMA7 EbMI7 Ab7 DbMA7 Gb7 C7 F+7
Bb7 Eb7 GMA7 BMI7 E7 AMA7 C#MI7 F#7
BMA7 BbMI7 Eb7 CMI7 F7(b9) BbMI7 Eb7(b9)
AbMA7 Bb7 BbMI7 Eb7 AbMA7
TO CODA
EbMI7 Ab7 DbMA7 Gb7 C7 F+7 BbMI7

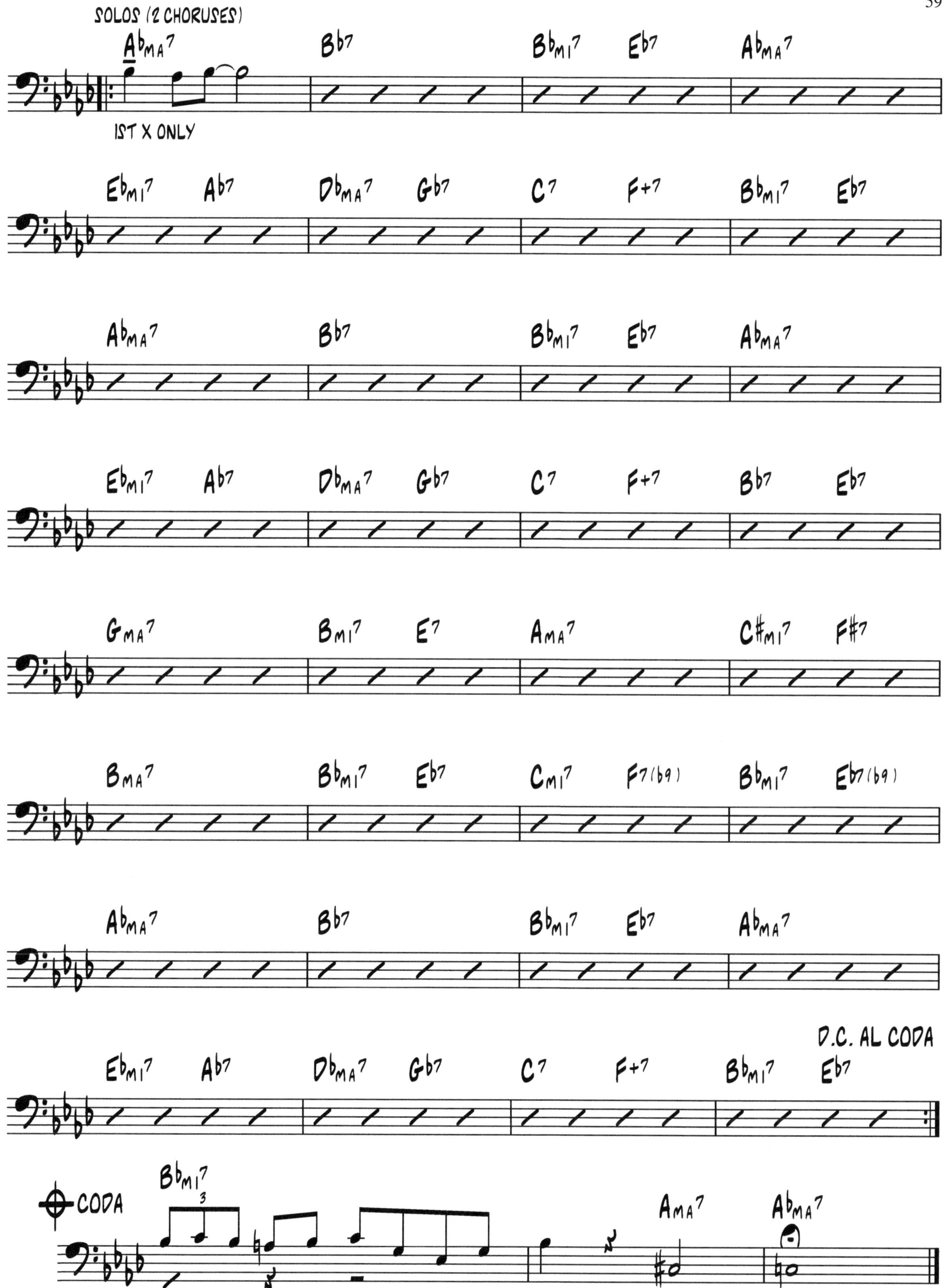
SOLOS (2 CHORUSES)
1ST X ONLY
D.C. AL CODA
CODA

RUDE OLD MAN

BY EUGENE WRIGHT

C VERSION

MEDIUM SWING

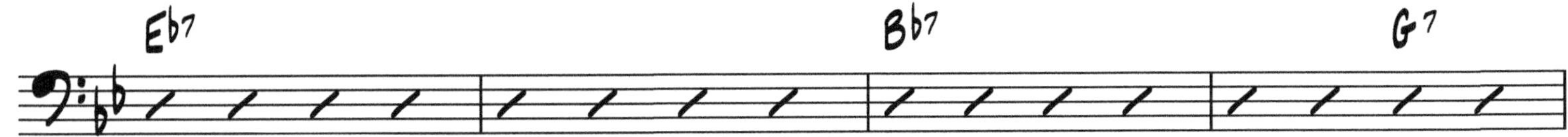

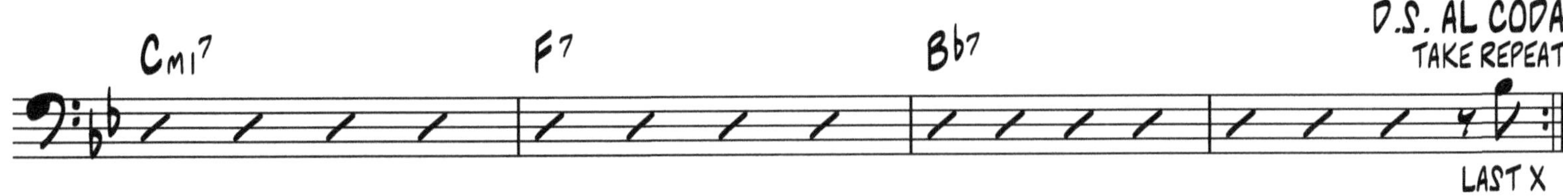

CD
13 : SPLIT TRACK/MELODY
14 : FULL STEREO TRACK

SUICIDE IS PAINLESS

(SONG FROM M*A*S*H)

WORDS AND MUSIC BY MIKE ALTMAN
AND JOHNNY MANDEL

𝄢: C VERSION

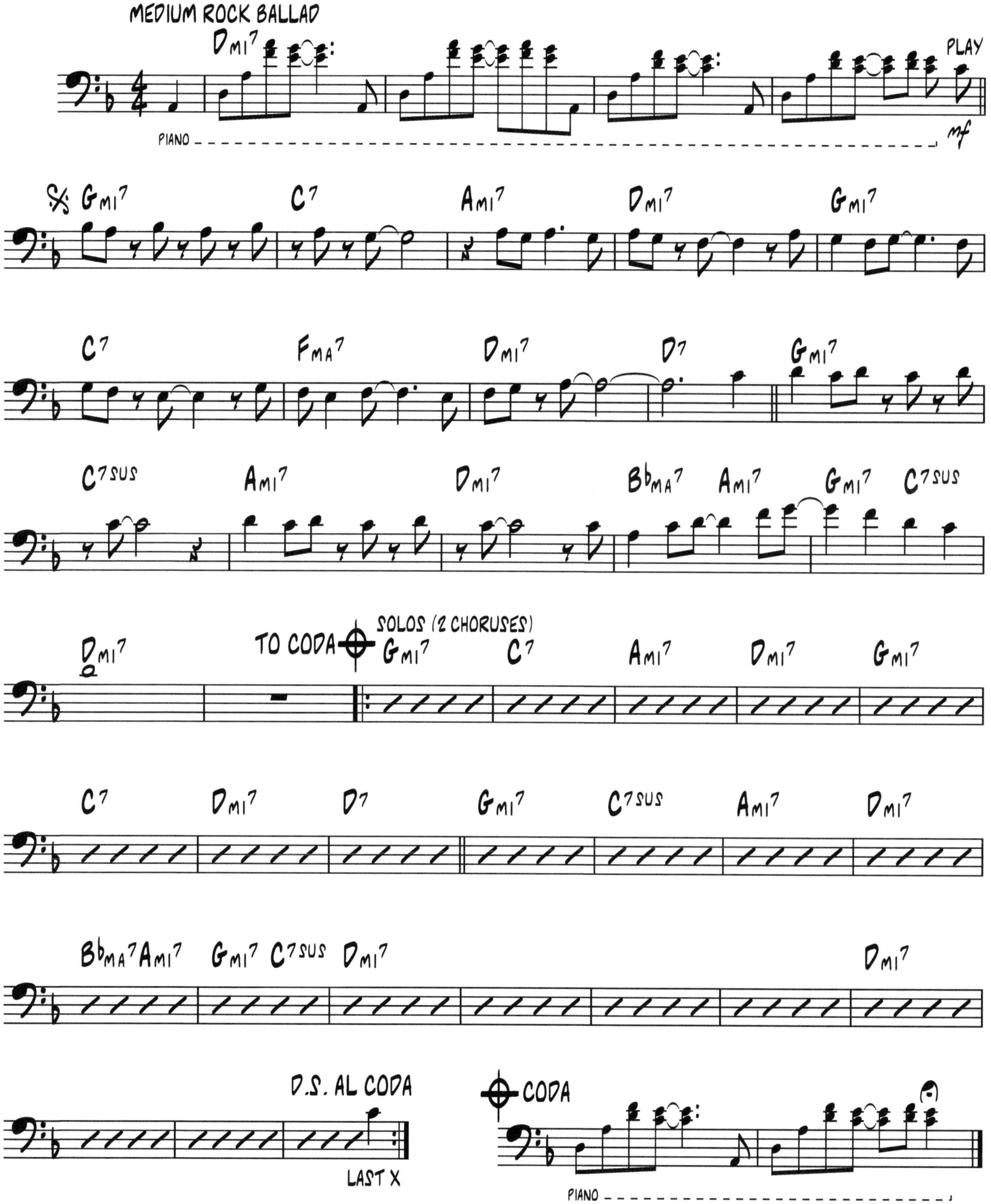

MEDIUM ROCK BALLAD

DMI7 PLAY
PIANO
mf

GMI7 C7 AMI7 DMI7 GMI7

C7 FMA7 DMI7 D7 GMI7

C7SUS AMI7 DMI7 B♭MA7 AMI7 GMI7 C7SUS

DMI7 TO CODA SOLOS (2 CHORUSES) GMI7 C7 AMI7 DMI7 GMI7

C7 DMI7 D7 GMI7 C7SUS AMI7 DMI7

B♭MA7 AMI7 GMI7 C7SUS DMI7 DMI7

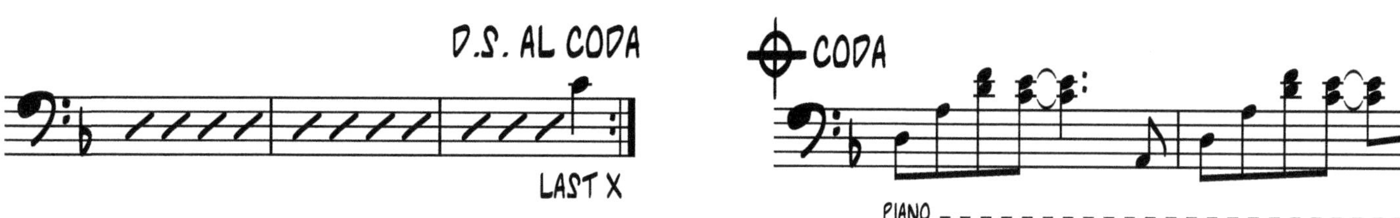

CD

9 : SPLIT TRACK/MELODY

10 : FULL STEREO TRACK

SAMBA CANTINA

BY PAUL DESMOND

TO CODA
Bbmi7 /Ab Gmi7(b5) C7 Fmi7 /Eb Bb7/D Bbmi6/Db
C7SUS
Fmi7
Ab7
SOLO
Gmi7(b5) C7 Fmi7 Bbmi7 Eb7
Abma7 Gmi7(b5) C7 Fmi7
Dmi7(b5) G7 C7 Ab7 Gmi7(b5) C7
Fmi7 Bbmi7 Eb7 Cmi7 F7
Bbmi7 /Ab Gmi7(b5) C7 Fmi7 /Eb Bb7/D Bbmi6/Db
C7SUS C7(b9) Fmi7
D.S. AL CODA
CODA C7SUS C7(b9) Fmi7 Fmi6 Fmi7
Fmi6 Fmi7 Fmi6 Fmi7 Fmi6/9

CD
11 : SPLIT TRACK/MELODY
12 : FULL STEREO TRACK

SAMBA DE ORFEU

WORDS BY ANTONIO MARIA
MUSIC BY LUIZ BONFA

𝄢: C VERSION

Fmi7
Bb7
Ebmi7
Ab7
Ebmi7
Ab7sus
Ab7
TO CODA
Ebmi7
Ab7
Dbma7
SOLO
Dbma7
Fmi7
Bb7
Ebmi7
Ab7
Ebmi7
Ab7sus
Ab7
Ebmi7
Ab7
1. Dbma7
Ab7sus
2. Dbma7
Abmi7
Db7
Gbma7
F#mi7
B7
Fmi7 Bb7
Ebmi7 Ab7sus
Dbma7
Fmi7
Bb7
Ebmi7
Ab7
Ebmi7
Ab7sus
Ab7
Ebmi7
Ab7
Dbma7
D.S. AL CODA
CODA
Ebmi7
Ab7
Db6/9
Ab7sus
Db6/9
Ab7sus
Db6/9
Ab7sus
Dbma7

TAKE FIVE

BY PAUL DESMOND

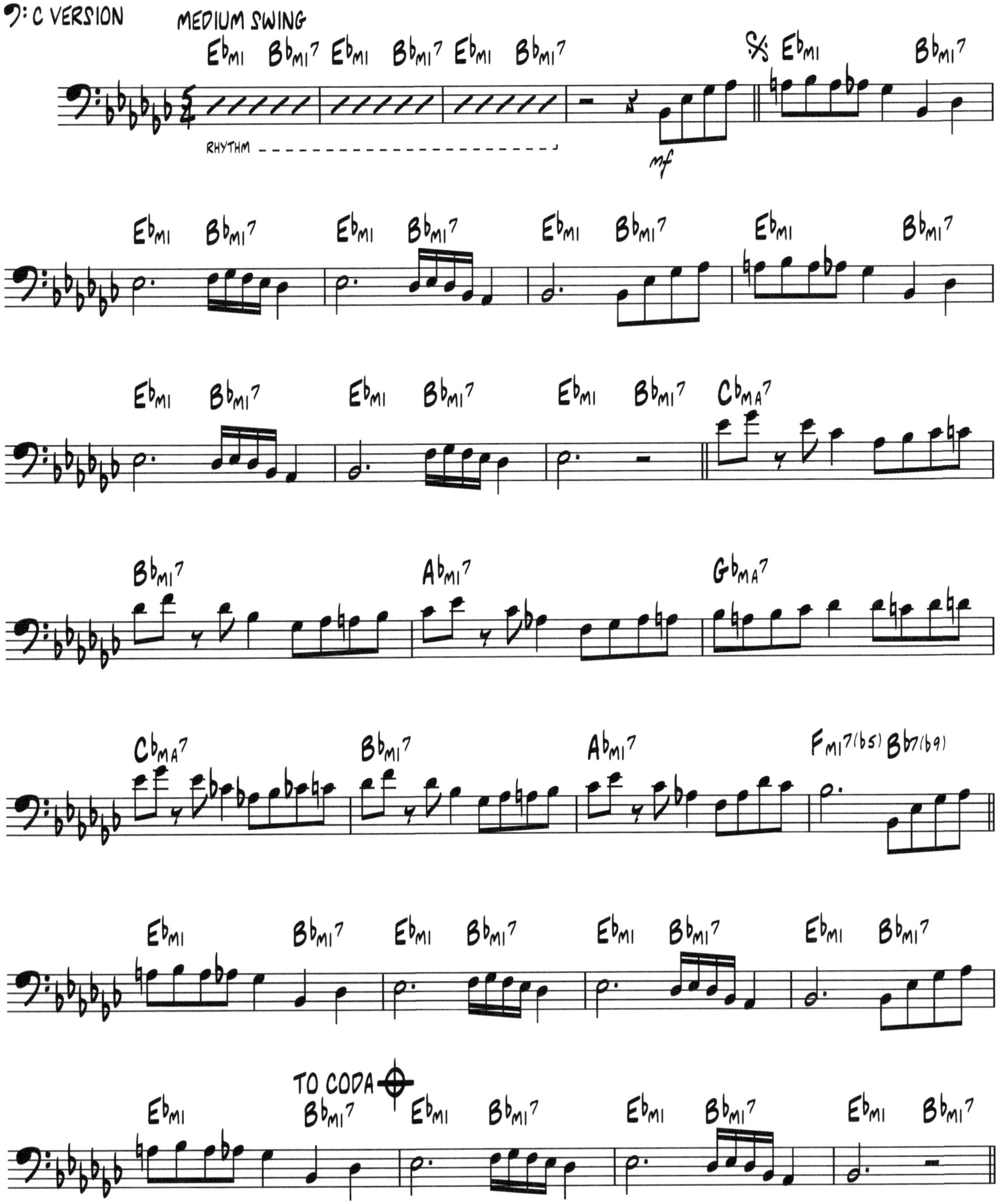

C VERSION

MEDIUM SWING

Ebmi Bbmi7 Ebmi Bbmi7 Ebmi Bbmi7 | 𝄋 Ebmi Bbmi7

RHYTHM

mf

Ebmi Bbmi7 Ebmi Bbmi7 Ebmi Bbmi7 Ebmi Bbmi7

Ebmi Bbmi7 Ebmi Bbmi7 Ebmi Bbmi7 Cbma7

Bbmi7 Abmi7 Gbma7

Cbma7 Bbmi7 Abmi7 Fmi7(b5) Bb7(b9)

Ebmi Bbmi7 Ebmi Bbmi7 Ebmi Bbmi7 Ebmi Bbmi7

TO CODA

Ebmi Bbmi7 Ebmi Bbmi7 Ebmi Bbmi7 Ebmi Bbmi7

SOLO
D.S. AL CODA
CODA

CD

17 : SPLIT TRACK/MELODY

18 : FULL STEREO TRACK

TAKE TEN

BY PAUL DESMOND

C VERSION

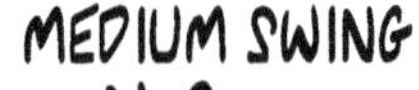

DMI7 G7 DMI7 G7 DMI7 G7 DMI7 G7

RHYTHM

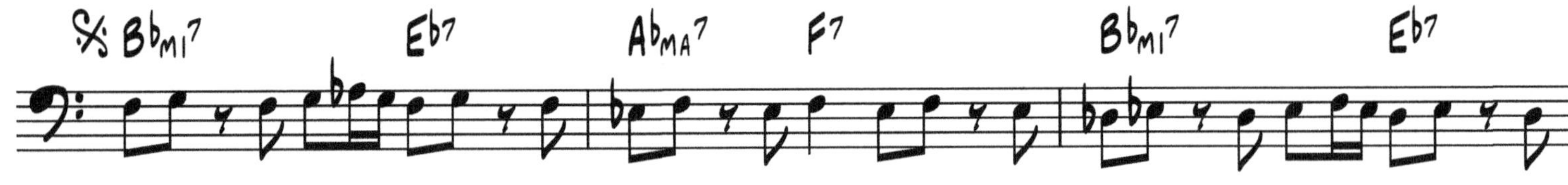

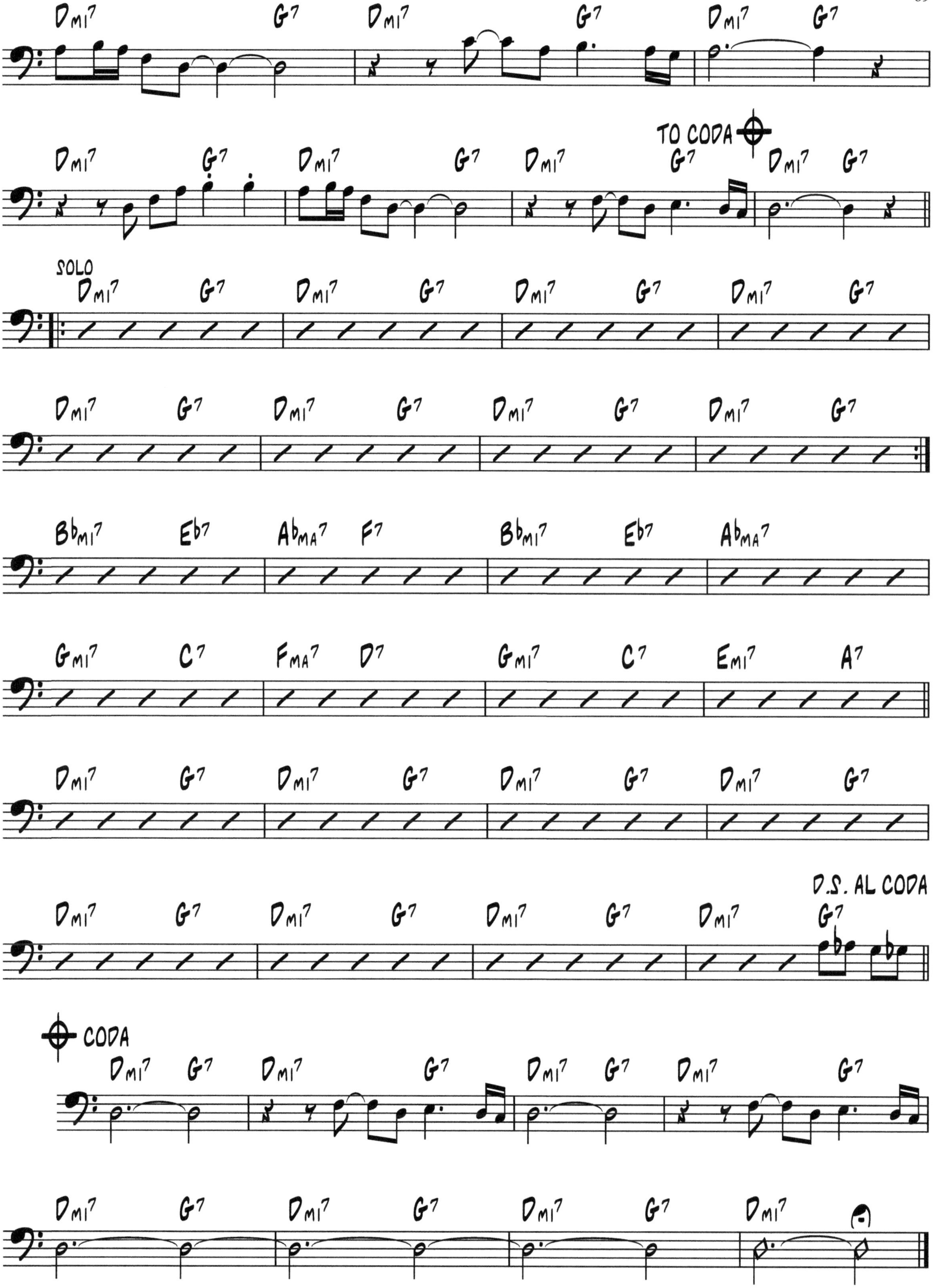
DMI7 G7 DMI7 G7 DMI7 G7
TO CODA
DMI7 G7 DMI7 G7 DMI7 G7 DMI7 G7
SOLO
DMI7 G7 DMI7 G7 DMI7 G7 DMI7 G7
DMI7 G7 DMI7 G7 DMI7 G7 DMI7 G7
Bbmi7 Eb7 AbMA7 F7 Bbmi7 Eb7 AbMA7
GMI7 C7 FMA7 D7 GMI7 C7 EMI7 A7
DMI7 G7 DMI7 G7 DMI7 G7 DMI7 G7
D.S. AL CODA
DMI7 G7 DMI7 G7 DMI7 G7 DMI7 G7
CODA
DMI7 G7 DMI7 G7 DMI7 G7 DMI7 G7
DMI7 G7 DMI7 G7 DMI7 G7 DMI7

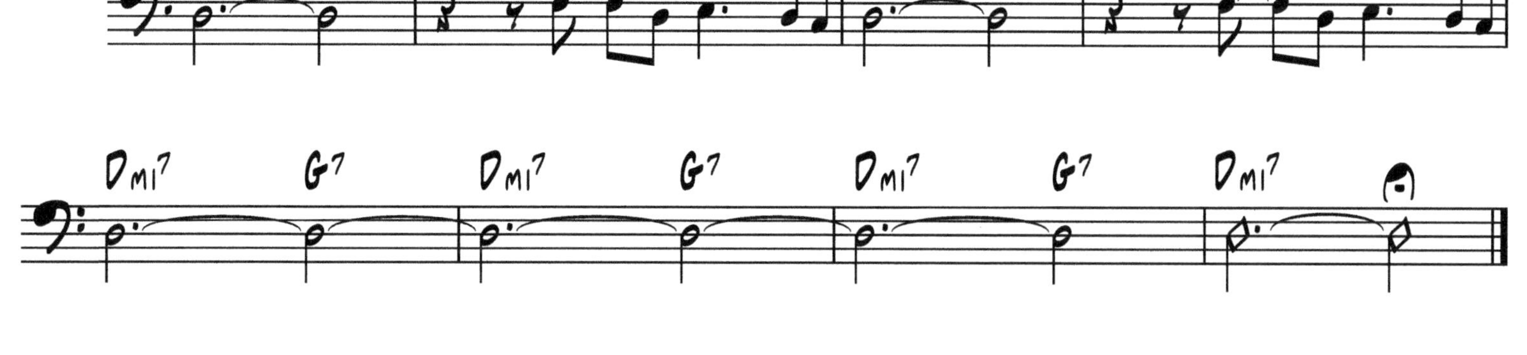

CD

19: SPLIT TRACK/MELODY
20: FULL STEREO TRACK

WHEN JOANNA LOVED ME

WORDS AND MUSIC BY ROBERT WELLS
AND JACK SEGAL

SOLO
Eb MA7
G MI7
C7(b9)
F MI7
Bb7
F MI7(b5)/Cb
Bb MI7
Eb7
Ab MA7
Ab MI7
A7
D7
C7
Bb7(b9)
E7
RIT.

90. **THELONIOUS MONK CLASSICS**
00841262 ....$16.99

91. **THELONIOUS MONK FAVORITES**
00841263....................$16.99

92. **LEONARD BERNSTEIN**
00450134....................$16.99

93. **DISNEY FAVORITES**
00843142....................$16.99

94. **RAY**
00843143....................$16.99

95. **JAZZ AT THE LOUNGE**
00843144....................$16.99

96. **LATIN JAZZ STANDARDS**
00843145....................$16.99

97. **MAYBE I'M AMAZED***
00843148....................$16.99

98. **DAVE FRISHBERG**
00843149....................$16.99

99. **SWINGING STANDARDS**
00843150....................$16.99

100. **LOUIS ARMSTRONG**
00740423....................$16.99

101. **BUD POWELL**
00843152....................$16.99

102. **JAZZ POP**
00843153....................$16.99

103. **ON GREEN DOLPHIN STREET & OTHER JAZZ CLASSICS**
00843154....................$16.99

104. **ELTON JOHN**
00843155....................$16.99

105. **SOULFUL JAZZ**
00843151....................$16.99

106. **SLO' JAZZ**
00843117....................$16.99

107. **MOTOWN CLASSICS**
00843116....................$16.99

108. **JAZZ WALTZ**
00843159....................$16.99

109. **OSCAR PETERSON**
00843160....................$16.99

110. **JUST STANDARDS**
00843161....................$16.99

111. **COOL CHRISTMAS**
00843162....................$16.99

112. **PAQUITO D'RIVERA – LATIN JAZZ***
48020662....................$16.99

113. **PAQUITO D'RIVERA – BRAZILIAN JAZZ***
48020663....................$19.99

114. **MODERN JAZZ QUARTET FAVORITES**
00843163....................$16.99

115. **THE SOUND OF MUSIC**
00843164....................$16.99

116. **JACO PASTORIUS**
00843165....................$16.99

117. **ANTONIO CARLOS JOBIM – MORE HITS**
00843166....................$16.99

118. **BIG JAZZ STANDARDS COLLECTION**
00843167....................$27.50

119. **JELLY ROLL MORTON**
00843168....................$16.99

120. **J.S. BACH**
00843169....................$16.99

121. **DJANGO REINHARDT**
00843170....................$16.99

122. **PAUL SIMON**
00843182....................$16.99

123. **BACHARACH & DAVID**
00843185....................$16.99

124. **JAZZ-ROCK HORN HITS**
00843186....................$16.99

125. **SAMMY NESTICO**
00843187....................$16.99

126. **COUNT BASIE CLASSICS**
00843157....................$16.99

127. **CHUCK MANGIONE**
00843188....................$16.99

128. **VOCAL STANDARDS (LOW VOICE)**
00843189....................$16.99

129. **VOCAL STANDARDS (HIGH VOICE)**
00843190....................$16.99

130. **VOCAL JAZZ (LOW VOICE)**
00843191....................$16.99

131. **VOCAL JAZZ (HIGH VOICE)**
00843192....................$16.99

132. **STAN GETZ ESSENTIALS**
00843193....................$16.99

133. **STAN GETZ FAVORITES**
00843194....................$16.99

134. **NURSERY RHYMES***
00843196....................$17.99

135. **JEFF BECK**
00843197....................$16.99

136. **NAT ADDERLEY**
00843198....................$16.99

137. **WES MONTGOMERY**
00843199....................$16.99

138. **FREDDIE HUBBARD**
00843200....................$16.99

139. **JULIAN "CANNONBALL" ADDERLEY**
00843201....................$16.99

140. **JOE ZAWINUL**
00843202....................$16.99

141. **BILL EVANS STANDARDS**
00843156....................$16.99

142. **CHARLIE PARKER GEMS**
00843222....................$16.99

143. **JUST THE BLUES**
00843223....................$16.99

144. **LEE MORGAN**
00843229....................$16.99

145. **COUNTRY STANDARDS**
00843230....................$16.99

146. **RAMSEY LEWIS**
00843231 ....$16.99

147. **SAMBA**
00843232 ....$16.99

148. **JOHN COLTRANE FAVORITES**
00843233....................$16.99

149. **JOHN COLTRANE – GIANT STEPS**
00843234....................$16.99

150. **JAZZ IMPROV BASICS**
00843195....................$19.99

151. **MODERN JAZZ QUARTET CLASSICS**
00843209....................$16.99

152. **J.J. JOHNSON**
00843210....................$16.99

153. **KENNY GARRETT**
00843212....................$16.99

154. **HENRY MANCINI**
00843213....................$16.99

155. **SMOOTH JAZZ CLASSICS**
00843215....................$16.99

156. **THELONIOUS MONK – EARLY GEMS**
00843216....................$16.99

157. **HYMNS**
00843217....................$16.99

158. **JAZZ COVERS ROCK**
00843219....................$16.99

159. **MOZART**
00843220....................$16.99

160. **GEORGE SHEARING**
14041531....................$16.99

161. **DAVE BRUBECK**
14041556 ....$16.99

162. **BIG CHRISTMAS COLLECTION**
00843221....................$24.99

163. **JOHN COLTRANE STANDARDS**
00843235....................$16.99

164. **HERB ALPERT**
14041775 ....$16.99

165. **GEORGE BENSON**
00843240....................$16.99

166. **ORNETTE COLEMAN**
00843241....................$16.99

167. **JOHNNY MANDEL**
00103642....................$16.99

168. **TADD DAMERON**
00103663....................$16.99

169. **BEST JAZZ STANDARDS**
00109249....................$19.99

170. **ULTIMATE JAZZ STANDARDS**
00109250....................$19.99

171. **RADIOHEAD**
00109305....................$16.99

172. **POP STANDARDS**
00111669....................$16.99

174. **TIN PAN ALLEY**
00119125....................$16.99

175. **TANGO**
00119836....................$16.99

176. **JOHNNY MERCER**
00119838....................$16.99

177. **THE II-V-I PROGRESSION**
00843239....................$19.99

178. **JAZZ/FUNK**
00121902....................$16.99

179. **MODAL JAZZ**
00122273....................$16.99

180. **MICHAEL JACKSON**
00122327....................$17.99

181. **BILLY JOEL**
00122329 ....$16.99

182. **"RHAPSODY IN BLUE" & 7 OTHER CLASSICAL-BASED JAZZ PIECES**
00116847....................$16.99

183. **SONDHEIM**
00126253....................$16.99

184. **JIMMY SMITH**
00126943....................$16.99

185. **JAZZ FUSION**
00127558....................$16.99

186. **JOE PASS**
00128391....................$16.99

187. **CHRISTMAS FAVORITES**
00128393....................$16.99

188. **PIAZZOLLA – 10 FAVORITE TUNES**
48023253....................$16.99

189. **JOHN LENNON**
00138678....................$16.99

0418

*These do not include split tracks.

JAZZ INSTRUCTION & IMPROVISATION

BOOKS FOR ALL INSTRUMENTS FROM HAL LEONARD

500 JAZZ LICKS

by Brent Vaartstra

This book aims to assist you on your journey to play jazz fluently. These short phrases and ideas we call "licks" will help you understand how to navigate the common chords and chord progressions you will encounter. Adding this vocabulary to your arsenal will send you down the right path and improve your jazz playing, regardless of your instrument.

00142384 .... $16.99

1001 JAZZ LICKS

by Jack Shneidman
Cherry Lane Music

This book presents 1,001 melodic gems played over dozens of the most important chord progressions heard in jazz. This is the ideal book for beginners seeking a well-organized, easy-to-follow encyclopedia of jazz vocabulary, as well as professionals who want to take their knowledge of the jazz language to new heights.

02500133 .... $14.99

THE BERKLEE BOOK OF JAZZ HARMONY

by Joe Mulholland & Tom Hojnacki

Learn jazz harmony, as taught at Berklee College of Music. This text provides a strong foundation in harmonic principles, supporting further study in jazz composition, arranging, and improvisation. It covers basic chord types and their tensions, with practical demonstrations of how they are used in characteristic jazz contexts and an accompanying recording that lets you hear how they can be applied.

00113755 Book/Online Audio $19.99

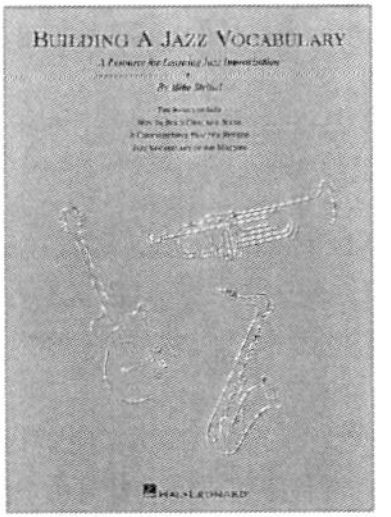

BUILDING A JAZZ VOCABULARY

By Mike Steinel

A valuable resource for learning the basics of jazz from Mike Steinel of the University of North Texas. It covers: the basics of jazz • how to build effective solos • a comprehensive practice routine • and a jazz vocabulary of the masters.

00849911 .... $19.99

COMPREHENSIVE TECHNIQUE FOR JAZZ MUSICIANS

2ND EDITION

by Bert Ligon
Houston Publishing

An incredible presentation of the most practical exercises an aspiring jazz student could want. All are logically interwoven with fine "real world" examples from jazz to classical. This book is an essential anthology of technical, compositional, and theoretical exercises, with lots of musical examples.

00030455 .... $34.99

EAR TRAINING

by Keith Wyatt, Carl Schroeder and Joe Elliott
Musicians Institute Press

Covers: basic pitch matching • singing major and minor scales • identifying intervals • transcribing melodies and rhythm • identifying chords and progressions • seventh chords and the blues • modal interchange, chromaticism, modulation • and more.

00695198 Book/Online Audio $24.99

EXERCISES AND ETUDES FOR THE JAZZ INSTRUMENTALIST

by J.J. Johnson

Designed as study material and playable by any instrument, these pieces run the gamut of the jazz experience, featuring common and uncommon time signatures and keys, and styles from ballads to funk. They are progressively graded so that both beginners and professionals will be challenged by the demands of this wonderful music.

00842018 Bass Clef Edition $19.99
00842042 Treble Clef Edition $16.95

HOW TO PLAY FROM A REAL BOOK

by Robert Rawlins

Explore, understand, and perform the songs in real books with the techniques in this book. Learn how to analyze the form and harmonic structure, insert an introduction, interpret the melody, improvise on the chords, construct bass lines, voice the chords, add substitutions, and more. It addresses many aspects of solo and small band performance that can improve your own playing and your understanding of what others are doing around you.

00312097 .... $19.99

JAZZ DUETS

ETUDES FOR PHRASING AND ARTICULATION

by Richard Lowell
Berklee Press

With these 27 duets in jazz and jazz-influenced styles, you will learn how to improve your ear, sense of timing, phrasing, and your facility in bringing theoretical principles into musical expression. Covers: jazz staccato & legato • scales, modes & harmonies • phrasing within and between measures • swing feel • and more.

00302151 .... $14.99

JAZZ THEORY & WORKBOOK

by Lilian Dericq & Étienne Guéreau

Designed for all instrumentalists, this book teaches how jazz standards are constructed. It is also a great resource for arrangers and composers seeking new writing tools. While some of the musical examples are pianistic, this book is not exclusively for keyboard players.

00159022 .... $19.99

JAZZ THEORY RESOURCES

by Bert Ligon
Houston Publishing, Inc.

This is a jazz theory text in two volumes. **Volume 1 includes:** review of basic theory • rhythm in jazz performance • triadic generalization • diatonic harmonic progressions and analysis • substitutions and turnarounds • and more. **Volume 2 includes**: modes and modal frameworks • quartal harmony • extended tertian structures and triadic superimposition • pentatonic applications • coloring "outside" the lines and beyond • and more.

00030458 Volume 1 .... $39.99
00030459 Volume 2 .... $32.99

JAZZOLOGY

THE ENCYCLOPEDIA OF JAZZ THEORY FOR ALL MUSICIANS

by Robert Rawlins and Nor Eddine Bahha

This comprehensive resource covers a variety of jazz topics, for beginners and pros of any instrument. The book serves as an encyclopedia for reference, a thorough methodology for the student, and a workbook for the classroom.

00311167 .... $24.99

MODALOGY

SCALES, MODES & CHORDS: THE PRIMORDIAL BUILDING BLOCKS OF MUSIC

by Jeff Brent with Schell Barkley

Primarily a music theory reference, this book presents a unique perspective on the origins, interlocking aspects, and usage of the most common scales and modes in occidental music. Anyone wishing to seriously explore the realms of scales, modes, and their real-world functions will find the most important issues dealt with in meticulous detail within these pages.

00312274 .... $24.99

THE SOURCE

THE DICTIONARY OF CONTEMPORARY AND TRADITIONAL SCALES

by Steve Barta

This book serves as an informative guide for people who are looking for good, solid information regarding scales, chords, and how they work together. It provides right and left hand fingerings for scales, chords, and complete inversions. Includes over 20 different scales, each written in all 12 keys.

00240885 .... $19.99

www.halleonard.com

Prices, contents & availability subject to change without notice.

0421
068

Transcribed Scores are vocal and instrumental arrangements of music from some of the greatest groups in music. These excellent publications feature transcribed parts for lead vocals, lead guitar, rhythm, guitar, bass, drums, and all of the various instruments used in each specific recording session. All songs are arranged exactly the way the artists recorded them.

00672527	**Audioslave**	$24.95
00673228	**The Beatles – Complete Scores** (Boxed Set)	$85.00
00672378	**The Beatles – Transcribed Scores**	$24.95
00673208	**Best of Blood, Sweat & Tears**	$19.95
00690636	**Best of Bluegrass**	$24.95
00672367	**Chicago – Volume 1**	$24.95
00672368	**Chicago – Volume 2**	$24.95
00672452	**Miles Davis – Birth of the Cool**	$24.95
00672460	**Miles Davis – Kind of Blue (Sketch Scores)**	$19.95
00672502	**Deep Purple – Greatest Hits**	$24.95
00672427	**Ben Folds Five – Selections from Naked Baby Photos**	$19.95
00672428	**Ben Folds Five – Whatever and Ever, Amen**	$19.95
00001333	**Getz/Gilberto**	$19.99
00672540	**Best of Good Charlotte**	$24.95
00672396	**The Don Grolnick Collection**	$17.95
02500361	**Guns N' Roses Greatest Hits**	$24.95
00672308	**Jimi Hendrix – Are You Experienced?**	$29.95
00672345	**Jimi Hendrix – Axis Bold As Love**	$29.95
00672313	**Jimi Hendrix – Band of Gypsys**	$29.95
00672397	**Jimi Hendrix – Experience Hendrix**	$29.95
00672500	**Best of Incubus**	$24.95
00672469	**Billy Joel Collection**	$24.95
00672415	**Eric Johnson – Ah Via Musicom**	$24.95
00672465	**John Lennon – Imagine**	$24.95
00672478	**The Best of Megadeth**	$24.95
02500424	**Best of Metallica**	$24.95
00672541	**Pat Metheny Group – The Way Up**	$19.95
02500883	**Mr. Big – Lean into It**	$24.95
00672504	**Gary Moore – Greatest Hits**	$24.95
00690582	**Nickel Creek – Nickel Creek**	$19.95
00690586	**Nickel Creek – This Side**	$19.95
00672545	**Nickel Creek – Why Should The Fire Die?**	$19.95
00672518	**Nirvana**	$24.95
00672403	**Nirvana – In Utero**	$24.95
00672404	**Nirvana – Incesticide**	$24.95
00672402	**Nirvana – Nevermind**	$24.95
00672405	**Nirvana – Unplugged in New York**	$24.95
00672466	**The Offspring – Americana**	$24.95
00672501	**The Police – Greatest Hits**	$24.95
00672538	**The Best of Queen**	$24.95
00672400	**Red Hot Chili Peppers – Blood Sugar Sex Magik**	$24.95
00672515	**Red Hot Chili Peppers – By the Way**	$24.95
00672456	**Red Hot Chili Peppers – Californication**	$24.95
00672536	**Red Hot Chili Peppers – Greatest Hits**	$24.95
00672422	**Red Hot Chili Peppers – Mother's Milk**	$24.95
00672551	**Red Hot Chili Peppers – Stadium Arcadium**	$49.95
00672408	**Rolling Stones – Exile on Main Street**	$24.95
00672360	**Santana's Greatest Hits**	$26.95
02500283	**Joe Satriani – Greatest Hits**	$24.95
00672522	**The Best of Slipknot**	$24.99
00675170	**The Best of Spyro Gyra**	$18.95
00675200	**The Best of Steely Dan**	$19.95
00672521	**Best of SUM 41**	$29.95
00675520	**Best of Weather Report**	$18.95

Prices, content, and availability subject to change without notice.

0212